better together*

*This book is best read together, grownup and kid.

 akidsco.com

a
kids
book
about

a
kids
book
about
Judaism
יהדות

by M.M. Friedman

A Kids Co.
Editor Emma Wolf
Designer Rick DeLucco
Creative Director Rick DeLucco
Studio Manager Kenya Feldes
Sales Director Melanie Wilkins
Head of Books Jennifer Goldstein
CEO and Founder Jelani Memory

DK
Delhi Technical Team Bimlesh Tiwary Pushpak Tyagi, Rakesh Kumar
Senior Production Editor Jennifer Murray
Senior Production Controller Louise Minihane
Senior Acquisitions Editor Katy Flint
Acquisitions Project Editor Sara Forster
Managing Art Editor Vicky Short
Managing Director, Licensing Mark Searle

First American edition, 2025
Published in the United States by DK Publishing, 1745 Broadway, 20th Floor,
New York, NY 10019

First published in Great Britain in 2025 by
Dorling Kindersley Limited, 20 Vauxhall Bridge Road, London SW1V 2SA
A Penguin Random House Company

The authorised representative in the EEA is
Dorling Kindersley Verlag GmbH. Arnulfstr. 124, 80636 Munich, Germany

A catalog record for this book is available from the Library of Congress.
A CIP catalogue record for this book is available from the British Library.
ISBN: 978-0-2417-4363-8

DK books are available at special discounts when purchased in bulk for sales
promotions, premiums, fund-raising, or education use. For details, contact
DK Publishing Special Markets, 1745 Broadway, 20th Floor, New York, NY 10019
SpecialSales@dk.com

Printed and bound in China
www.dk.com
akidsco.com

MIX
Paper | Supporting
responsible forestry
FSC™ C018179

This book was made with Forest
Stewardship Council™ certified
paper – one small step in DK's
commitment to a sustainable future.
**Learn more at www.dk.com/uk/
information/sustainability**

To every kid out there questioning, learning, growing, and discovering the world around them.

Intro
for grownups

It isn't difficult to find information about Jewish people. A lot of both positive and negative information exists describing one of the smallest, but historically first, monotheistic religions out there. Where should parents turn to teach kids about the joys and beauty of Orthodox Judaism?

This book is here to give you a brief introduction and short overview about where the Jewish people originated, some of the laws and traditions still honored today, and how kindness, compassion, and being empathetic to others are all at the core of what it means to be Jewish.

This book is here for grownups and kids to learn more about Judaism, as well as to discover and be proud of their Jewish heritage.

Hi, my name is Menachem Friedman and I'm from Brooklyn, New York.

Almost everyone calls me Mendy— I hope you will too.

This is a book about **Judaism**.

If I wrote a book that told you everything about Judaism, it might take a whole lifetime to read.

But we just don't have that much time!

So let's start with the basics...

What is Judaism?

Judaism is a religion.

Those who practice Judaism believe there is 1 God only and that this God provides a way of life that is fulfilling and kind.

We also believe God gave
the **Torah** תּוֹרָה (**toh-ruh**)
to the Jewish people.

The Torah is written in an
ancient language still spoken
today called Hebrew.

The Torah contains all the ways, rules, ethics, and traditions for us to live by, which are called **mitzvahs** מִצְווֹת **(mitz-vahs).***

*There are 613 mitzvahs, to be exact.

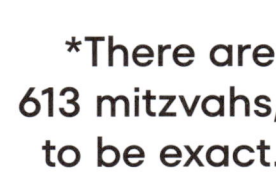

I can't remember a time when Judaism wasn't essential to every part of my life.

I was born and raised in an Orthodox Jewish community.

I have 4 siblings (I'm in the middle) and a mom and a dad.

I went to a religious Jewish school called Yeshivah, where we studied ancient Hebrew and learned how to pray in Hebrew too.

I also did ordinary things
that most other kids do like...

- Read books.

- Go to summer camp.

- Eat lots of ice cream.

- And I loved watching baseball—go, Yankees!

One of the mitzvahs we practice is **Shabbos** שַׁבָּת **(Shahb-bos),** also called Shabbat.

Shabbos happens
every week for 24 hours.

Yes, every single week.

It begins Friday night
at sundown and lasts until
Saturday night at nightfall.

Jewish people believe that Shabbos is a day of rest because when God created the world, he rested on the 7th day.

So, for us, that means...

- **no work for grownups,**

- **no iPads or screen time for kids,**

- **no cooking, cleaning, or electrical devices for anyone,**

- **and definitely no homework—yay!**

What happens on Shabbos?

Families come together
to share a special meal.

You get to be with all the people you
love most without any distractions.

There is prayer, singing, games,
conversation, and lots of joy.

(It's kind of like having Thanksgiving every weekend!)

Many parts of my life as an observant Jewish person might sound different or new to you.

Like, did you know
I only eat kosher food?

Kosher literally means "genuine or proper."

So, eating kosher means I only eat certain foods in specific ways.

Some of the foods I do not eat are pork, bacon, crab, lobster, or other seafood.

There are some foods I can eat, but just not in combination.

Like, I don't eat any meat with milk.

(That's a fancy way of saying no cheeseburgers.)

But don't feel sad for me! Almost anywhere you find Jewish people, you can find great kosher food to eat.

Just look for the kosher labels on food packaging!

You might be asking yourself,

Why do Jewish people eat kosher food and celebrate Shabbos?

Because we believe this is what God wants us to do, and that's really important to us.

Jewish people have been carefully keeping these traditions for thousands of years and passing them down from grownups to kids for generations.

Throughout history, Jewish people have sometimes had to quit jobs or lose customers in order to respect our religious laws, like closing our stores or businesses every Shabbos.

We do it because our parents
and ancestors did it before us.

It's a way of keeping
our traditions alive.

They are a part of who we are.

And there are so many other practices that are a part of my everyday life and Jewish identity.

I pray 3 times a day—in the morning, in the afternoon, and at night.

I wear a **kippah** כיפה (kip-pah) or **yarmulke** (YAH-mi-koh) on my head every day.

I learn Torah whenever I can.

And there are holidays
to celebrate, like

Passover פֶּסַח,

Hannakuh חֲנֻכָּה
(Chaa-nuh-ka),

Rosh Hashanah רֹאשׁ הַשָּׁנָה
(Row-shh Ha-sha-na),

Yom Kippur יוֹם כִּפּוּר
(Yom Kip-pur),

and Purim פּוּרִים
(Poo-reem).

Some of these holidays are really fun and you get great gifts **(like on Hanukkah)**, and on others you get to dress up, wear costumes, and give out lots of candy **(like Purim)**!

Some of these holidays include the Jewish New Year **(Rosh Hashanah)** and the holiest day of the year where we pray and fast **(Yom Kippur)**.

We celebrate when young people turn 12 or 13 with a huge party, dancing, and reading from the Torah, to symbolize growing up and becoming responsible for keeping God's commandments.

Remember when I told you there was too much about Judaism to fit in 1 book?

This is what I mean!

So, who are the

They are the descendants of

Jewish People?

Abraham, Isaac, and Jacob.

Long ago, Jewish people were enslaved in Egypt for many years.

God eventually freed them and took them out of Egypt.

And God gave the
Torah to Moses and
the Jewish people on Mt. Sinai.

Thousands of years ago, Jews lived in their ancestral home of Israel, where the temple stood in Jerusalem.

Today, 1 wall of that holy temple still stands—I was lucky enough to visit once!

Because of the long history of Judaism, Jews can be found almost anywhere and everywhere.

In fact, there are about 14 million Jews around the world.*

*If you're curious whether you're Jewish, look to your mother's side of the family! Judaism is a matrilineal religion, so follow the ancestry of your mother to find out if that's a part of your story too!

Throughout history,
Jewish people have been
persecuted* just for being Jewish.

So, they have had to move
to many new places to find
a peaceful and better life.

*Persecuted means
 discriminated against, hated, and treated unfairly.

That means you can find Jewish people in almost every size, shape, color, or country.

You can find different Jewish cuisine, cultures, and even languages based on where they come from.

According to the Torah,
all people were created
in God's image.

Which means that all people have inherent goodness and deserve to be treated with respect and kindness.

The Jewish people believe that the values of being kind, respecting our parents and our elders, giving to charities, helping others, and loving your neighbor are all essential to Judaism.

This is called Chessed חֶסֶד,
(Che-sed).

Chessed is all about doing good deeds and helping others.

Which is what I strive to do every day.

Judaism is about living for a higher purpose and bringing joy and a sense of mission to our lives.

I'm not perfect and don't always get it right, but I'm trying.

And I'm thankful to my many friends, family, community, rabbis, and God, who help me on this journey.

Outro
for grownups

Now that you know what Judaism is and the different ways to celebrate it, there are many ways to continue educating yourself about Judaism and learn more about Jewish people.

Grownups, this is the time to share your experiences with either being Jewish or those around you who are Jewish, and what this religion means and how it has impacted you.

This is also a good time to teach kids about religious persecution, baseless hatred, and how it has impacted lots of religions worldwide. By learning about religions and groups other than our own, we discover the beauty and similarities between us that we never knew existed, which create a more meaningful, equal, and diverse world.

About The Author

M. M. Friedman (he/him) wrote this book for any kid or parent out there discovering or wanting to discover their Jewish heritage. Growing up Jewish and religious in faith, he wanted to display the beauty, depth, and possible fun of one of the world's most famous but minuscule religions.

M. M. Friedman has visited many countries and traveled the world to see how different Jewish cultures live, pray, and interact with one another, trying new foods and experiencing new customs along the way.

This book is meant to be a beginner's guide to Judaism for both grownups and kids, describing some of the practices and holidays Jewish people honor, as well as offering outsiders a newfound understanding and, ultimately, appreciation of the Jewish people.

Made to empower.

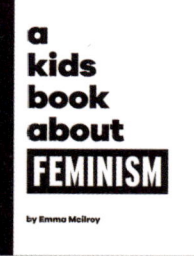

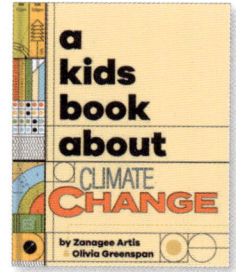